MENTAL DYNAMIC REVIEW

# MENTAL SCORES

TENNIS

Heiko Hansen

MENTAL SCORES TENNIS / Mental Dynamic Review
ISBN: 978-3-7481-6706-8
Production and publishing: Book on Demand GmbH, Norderstedt / Germany
1st edition (2018)
Copyright: Heiko Hansen

MENTAL DYNAMIC REVIEW

# MENTAL SCORES

TENNIS

NAME

_____

Season 20___/___

# Table of Contents

*If you have passed the MiD Test (Mental Implicit Dynamic: ViQ® or PST® Test), please note the following data here:*

**Name:** _____

Shirt nummer _____    Club _____

Season  20 ___ /___    Date of MiD-Test: _____

## MiD Code (ViQ® or PST®)

My mental implicit priority / First dynamic, f.e. SO.1

| Recognation priority (S or A) | Memory- priority (O or P) | Motivation orientation 1/2/3 oder 4 |
|---|---|---|
|  |  |  |

Please note the characteristic values here:

| S | A | O | P | Sti | Sic |
|---|---|---|---|---|---|
|  |  |  |  |  |  |

*www.mentaldynamic.info*

## MD Profiling Comments

If you would like an evaluation interview with a certified
MD Profiler, then please note your most important
Insights and comments for your sporting mental success!

## MD seasonal goals

which I want to achieve or learn. Set yourself one season goal for each theme, at most two goals. It's not about the amount of goals, but about the development of meaningful things to constancy.

### Tactically

### Technically

### Athletic

### Mentally

This is how I want to perform mentally, act mentally in a game/game or tennis tournament.

My self-responsibility, or rather, I do this on my own commitment in order to play successfully.

That's what I expect from my trainer (team). That's important for me!

**Signature Me / Player**                    **Signature Coach**

10

# Important notes

## 1 / Items

From my more than 25 years of experience, I have defined the most important mental criteria that determine mental performance. Ultimately, it's all about success in the competition and showing your talent and potential in a sustainable way. The feeling of having achieved, if not exceeded, one's performance is another than having failed.

It is primarily about learning success through a fair review: for an attentive, recognizing development and the view of the momentum. And: It's about a basis for discussion and knowledge that should enable the development of mental talent for a successful overall performance.

**1a /** In consultation between player/athlete and coach, the given criteria can be changed or exchanged and/or up to three additional criteria can be entered.

Please enter the item "Teamspirit" for double games in addition.

This also applies to tennis specific items/goals you are working on or which are very important to you such as effectiveness of forehand / backhand, baseline play.

Another reason can be special mental goals for the season, e.g. those resulting from the MiD test or for the mental training of meaning are.

**1b /** After each game / competition please enter the **winner-item** (best rated) and the **loser-item** in the season performance. This gives you a quick overview of your mental strengths and what you still have to work on.

### 1c / Tactical implementation

Tactical task reliably fulfilled / acting in momentum / behaviour during tactical change / tactical ideas - solutions

### 1d / Self-activation / power

Energy potential fully exploited / everything given / willingness and joy to perform / pushes yourself (self-talk) / activation in the half-time break or before the game

### 1e / Focus and concentration

Attention level / sustainable or changing phases

### 1f / Emotion control

Emotional stability / creativity - surprising actions / dealing with fear or provocation

### 1g / Fighting Spirit

Two-fight leadership / has fought back / has asserted / acted with courage / effective aggressiveness / opponent - opponent impressed

### 1h / Competition setting

Self-development of a positive competitive mood / desire will to win (grade 1 - 2)

**or** rather fear / scepticism / insecure charisma / stage fright too high (grades 3 - 4)

### 1i / Action safety

Effectiveness / cleverness / decisions made correctly / high self-efficacy / personal initiative

### 1j / Mental stability

Mentally strong and stable under pressure / dealing with mistakes and unsuccessful actions / not provocative / good emotion regulation

### 1k / Body language

Positive charisma / head up / down / expression of self-doubt / giving up

### 1l / Pause effectiveness

Self-regulation between the blows, e.g. ritual or Breathing / self-talk / target effectiveness for the coming stroke

### Add extra / Teamspirit (Double)

Coached and helped fellow players / Team support / Corrections given / Direct communication and contact with fellow players.

## 2 / Rating (grades)

For me, notes are a form of evaluation and serve to orient the performance shown. They do not mean the absolute truth. Our sensory perception and evaluation system are too weak for this. Video studies are also helpful accordingly.

Personally I recommend a grading system of 1-2-3-4. The criteria must be clear: when is a 1 a 1, when is a 2 a 2. The grading feeling is different in people, e.g. how strictly one grades.

**For orientation I recommend:**

Grade 1 is very good and reflects a perfect performance of 90-100% reflected.

Grade 2 between 80-90%.

Grade 3 between 70-80%.

Grade 4 is below 70%.

After internal arrangement you can also between evalua-
tions
in 0.5 steps: 1.5 / 2.5 / 3.5.
1,5 = 95% / 2,5 = 85% / 3,5 = 75%.

## 3 / Third evaluator

Beside the own evaluation and by the (co-)trainer a third
person should evaluate the mental performance, e.g. parent
part, mental trainer, club scout, consultant or also interesting
a fellow player.

The third person can or should change from game to game.
Therefore, the field for entering the name has remained
white. The third evaluator can be entered alternately. Changing the name makes sense: It can easily lead to a 2:1 opponent ratio. If two evaluators are too critical or uncritical, the
feedback will not achieve the learning goal.

## 4 / Meaning of the two average grades

**4a /** On the right the average score of the ratings for the
respective item is noted, e.g. "tactical implementation":
I/player = 2 / Trainer = 1 / 3.evaluator = 2, gives an average
score of 1,67.

**4b /** The game score must be entered at the bottom.
It results from the average of all items.

## 5 / NOTE 1

The evaluation approaches are different. You have to
calibrate yourself in the criteria (see note 2). Otherwise it will
quickly lead to discord and misunderstanding between you.

Some scorers are too low/pampering, some too high/strict. Some people are more (self-)critical (perfectionists), some are more careless. All the more important is the calibration of the evaluation standards.

Much is gained when the use of this tool leads to more balance/clarity in the moment, profitable discussions and to more self-responsibility for the own talent development leads. This also applies to the trainer and his own trainer talents.

Let us best follow the path of the shining eyes (pure motivation), curiosity and openness for learning. But you don't have to be able to do everything. Nobody is perfect. Mistakes belong to life and are to be understood as 'helpers'. AND not to forget: Mistakes are specialists to support you.

## 6 / NOTE 2

Please clarify all items and evaluation approaches BEFORE you start the performance evaluation.

## 7 / NOTE 3

Use this tool seriously and sustainably. All the more success and clarity it will bring.

## 8 / MENTAL MASTER

To intensify the use of the mental dynamic score, you can choose or award one Mental Master per game/game or competition, per month and/or per season as a trainer/club.

# My Season Performance / Mental Scores

| GAMES | ME | Coa ch | 3.Per son | Winner-Item | Loser-Item |
|---|---|---|---|---|---|
| Game 1 | | | | | |
| Game 2 | | | | | |
| Game 3 | | | | | |
| Game 4 | | | | | |
| Game 5 | | | | | |
| Game 6 | | | | | |
| Game 7 | | | | | |
| Game 8 | | | | | |
| Game 9 | | | | | |
| Game 10 | | | | | |
| Game 11 | | | | | |
| Game 12 | | | | | |
| Game 13 | | | | | |
| Game 14 | | | | | |
| Game 15 | | | | | |
| Game 16 | | | | | |
| **Average** | | | | | |

| GAMES | Me | Coach | 3.Person | Winner-Item | Loser-Item |
|---|---|---|---|---|---|
| Game 17 | | | | | |
| Game 18 | | | | | |
| Game 19 | | | | | |
| Game 20 | | | | | |
| Game 21 | | | | | |
| Game 22 | | | | | |
| Game 23 | | | | | |
| Game 24 | | | | | |
| Game 25 | | | | | |
| Game 26 | | | | | |
| Game 27 | | | | | |
| Game 28 | | | | | |
| Game 29 | | | | | |
| Game 30 | | | | | |
| Game 31 | | | | | |
| Game 32 | | | | | |
| **Average** | | | | | |

| GAMES | Me | Coach | 3.Person | Winner-Item | Loser-Item |
|---|---|---|---|---|---|
| Game 33 | | | | | |
| Game 34 | | | | | |
| Game 35 | | | | | |
| Game 36 | | | | | |
| Game 37 | | | | | |
| Game 38 | | | | | |
| Game 39 | | | | | |
| Game 40 | | | | | |
| Game 41 | | | | | |
| Game 42 | | | | | |
| Game 43 | | | | | |
| Game 44 | | | | | |
| Game 45 | | | | | |
| Game 46 | | | | | |
| Game 47 | | | | | |
| Game 48 | | | | | |
| **Average** | | | | | |

**Important comments**

**Goals for the next season**

# Game / Competition 1 _____

Date: _____    Play time: _____ H/Min

O League Game    O Cup Game    O International / CL / EL

O National Team    O Practice Game    O Test-/Pre Season Game

| Items | Me | Coach | | Average |
|---|---|---|---|---|
| Tactical implementation | | | | |
| Selfactivating / Power | | | | |
| Focus / Concentration | | | | |
| Courageous, self-confident action | | | | |
| Fighting Spirit | | | | |
| Competition setting | | | | |
| Action / handling security | | | | |
| Mental stability | | | | |
| Body language | | | | |
| Pause effectiveness | | | | |
| | | | | |
| | | | | |
| | | | | |
| | | | | |
| **Mental Score / Average** | | | | |

**Important comments**

**Goal(s) for the upcoming training week**

**Goal(s) for the upcoming game/competition**

# Game / Competition 2 _____

Date: _____          Play time: _____ H/Min

○ League Game     ○ Cup Game     ○ International / CL / EL

○ National Team     ○ Practice Game     ○ Test-/Pre Season Game

| Items | Me | Coach | | Average |
|---|---|---|---|---|
| Tactical implementation | | | | |
| Selfactivating / Power | | | | |
| Focus / Concentration | | | | |
| Courageous, self-confident action | | | | |
| Fighting Spirit | | | | |
| Competition setting | | | | |
| Action / handling security | | | | |
| Mental stability | | | | |
| Body language | | | | |
| Pause effectiveness | | | | |
| | | | | |
| | | | | |
| | | | | |
| | | | | |
| **Mental Score /** Average | | | | |

© HeikoHansen.de

**Important comments**

**Goal(s) for the upcoming training week**

**Goal(s) for the upcoming game/competition**

# Game / Competition 3 _____

Date: _____        Play time: _____ H/Min

O League Game    O Cup Game    O International / CL / EL

O National Team    O Practice Game    O Test-/Pre Season Game

| Items | Me | Coach | | Average |
|---|---|---|---|---|
| Tactical implementation | | | | |
| Selfactivating / Power | | | | |
| Focus / Concentration | | | | |
| Courageous, self-confident action | | | | |
| Fighting Spirit | | | | |
| Competition setting | | | | |
| Action / handling security | | | | |
| Mental stability | | | | |
| Body language | | | | |
| Pause effectiveness | | | | |
| | | | | |
| | | | | |
| | | | | |
| | | | | |
| **Mental Score / Average** | | | | |

**Important comments**

**Goal(s) for the upcoming training week**

**Goal(s) for the upcoming game/competition**

# Game / Competition 4 _____

Date: _____  Play time: _____ H/Min

O League Game   O Cup Game   O International / CL / EL

O National Team   O Practice Game   O Test-/Pre Season Game

| Items | Me | Coach | | Average |
|---|---|---|---|---|
| Tactical implementation | | | | |
| Selfactivating / Power | | | | |
| Focus / Concentration | | | | |
| Courageous, self-confident action | | | | |
| Fighting Spirit | | | | |
| Competition setting | | | | |
| Action / handling security | | | | |
| Mental stability | | | | |
| Body language | | | | |
| Pause effectiveness | | | | |
| | | | | |
| | | | | |
| | | | | |
| | | | | |
| **Mental Score / Average** | | | | |

**Important comments**

**Goal(s) for the upcoming training week**

**Goal(s) for the upcoming game/competition**

# Game / Competition 5 _____

Date: _____     Play time: _____ H/Min

O League Game     O Cup Game     O International / CL / EL

O National Team     O Practice Game     O Test-/Pre Season Game

| Items | Me | Coach | | Average |
|---|---|---|---|---|
| Tactical implementation | | | | |
| Selfactivating / Power | | | | |
| Focus / Concentration | | | | |
| Courageous, self-confident action | | | | |
| Fighting Spirit | | | | |
| Competition setting | | | | |
| Action / handling security | | | | |
| Mental stability | | | | |
| Body language | | | | |
| Pause effectiveness | | | | |
| | | | | |
| | | | | |
| | | | | |
| | | | | |
| **Mental Score / Average** | | | | |

**Important comments**

**Goal(s) for the upcoming training week**

**Goal(s) for the upcoming game/competition**

# Game / Competition 6 _____

Date: _____     Play time: _____ H/Min

O League Game    O Cup Game    O International / CL / EL

O National Team    O Practice Game    O Test-/Pre Season Game

| Items | Me | Coach | | Average |
|---|---|---|---|---|
| Tactical implementation | | | | |
| Selfactivating / Power | | | | |
| Focus / Concentration | | | | |
| Courageous, self-confident action | | | | |
| Fighting Spirit | | | | |
| Competition setting | | | | |
| Action / handling security | | | | |
| Mental stability | | | | |
| Body language | | | | |
| Pause effectiveness | | | | |
| | | | | |
| | | | | |
| | | | | |
| | | | | |
| **Mental Score / Average** | | | | |

**Important comments**




**Goal(s) for the upcoming training week**




**Goal(s) for the upcoming game/competition**

# Game / Competition 7 _____

Date: _____     Play time: _____ H/Min

○ League Game    ○ Cup Game    ○ International / CL / EL

○ National Team    ○ Practice Game    ○ Test-/Pre Season Game

| Items | Me | Coach | | Average |
|---|---|---|---|---|
| Tactical implementation | | | | |
| Selfactivating / Power | | | | |
| Focus / Concentration | | | | |
| Courageous, self-confident action | | | | |
| Fighting Spirit | | | | |
| Competition setting | | | | |
| Action / handling security | | | | |
| Mental stability | | | | |
| Body language | | | | |
| Pause effectiveness | | | | |
| | | | | |
| | | | | |
| | | | | |
| | | | | |
| **Mental Score / Average** | | | | |

**Important comments**

**Goal(s) for the upcoming training week**

**Goal(s) for the upcoming game/competition**

# Game / Competition 8 _____

Date: _____  Play time: _____ H/Min

○ League Game   ○ Cup Game   ○ International / CL / EL

○ National Team   ○ Practice Game   ○ Test-/Pre Season Game

| Items | Me | Coach | Average |
|---|---|---|---|
| Tactical implementation | | | |
| Selfactivating / Power | | | |
| Focus / Concentration | | | |
| Courageous, self-confident action | | | |
| Fighting Spirit | | | |
| Competition setting | | | |
| Action / handling security | | | |
| Mental stability | | | |
| Body language | | | |
| Pause effectiveness | | | |
| | | | |
| | | | |
| | | | |
| | | | |
| **Mental Score / Average** | | | |

© HeikoHansen.de

**Important comments**

**Goal(s) for the upcoming training week**

**Goal(s) for the upcoming game/competition**

# Game / Competition 9 _____

Date: _____          Play time: _____ H/Min

O League Game     O Cup Game     O International / CL / EL

O National Team     O Practice Game     O Test-/Pre Season Game

| Items | Me | Coach | | Average |
|---|---|---|---|---|
| Tactical implementation | | | | |
| Selfactivating / Power | | | | |
| Focus / Concentration | | | | |
| Courageous, self-confident action | | | | |
| Fighting Spirit | | | | |
| Competition setting | | | | |
| Action / handling security | | | | |
| Mental stability | | | | |
| Body language | | | | |
| Pause effectiveness | | | | |
| | | | | |
| | | | | |
| | | | | |
| | | | | |
| **Mental Score** / Average | | | | |

**Important comments**

**Goal(s) for the upcoming training week**

**Goal(s) for the upcoming game/competition**

# Game / Competition 10 _____

Date: _____  Play time: _____ H/Min

O League Game  O Cup Game  O International / CL / EL

O National Team  O Practice Game  O Test-/Pre Season Game

| Items | Me | Coach | | Average |
|---|---|---|---|---|
| Tactical implementation | | | | |
| Selfactivating / Power | | | | |
| Focus / Concentration | | | | |
| Courageous, self-confident action | | | | |
| Fighting Spirit | | | | |
| Competition setting | | | | |
| Action / handling security | | | | |
| Mental stability | | | | |
| Body language | | | | |
| Pause effectiveness | | | | |
| | | | | |
| | | | | |
| | | | | |
| | | | | |
| **Mental Score / Average** | | | | |

**Important comments**




**Goal(s) for the upcoming training week**




**Goal(s) for the upcoming game/competition**

# Game / Competition 11 _____

Date: _____          Play time: _____ H/Min

O League Game     O Cup Game     O International / CL / EL

O National Team     O Practice Game     O Test-/Pre Season Game

| Items | Me | Coach | | Average |
|---|---|---|---|---|
| Tactical implementation | | | | |
| Selfactivating / Power | | | | |
| Focus / Concentration | | | | |
| Courageous, self-confident action | | | | |
| Fighting Spirit | | | | |
| Competition setting | | | | |
| Action / handling security | | | | |
| Mental stability | | | | |
| Body language | | | | |
| Pause effectiveness | | | | |
| | | | | |
| | | | | |
| | | | | |
| | | | | |
| **Mental Score / Average** | | | | |

© HeikoHansen.de

**Important comments**

**Goal(s) for the upcoming training week**

**Goal(s) for the upcoming game/competition**

# Game / Competition 12 _____

Date: _____ Play time: _____ H/Min

O League Game     O Cup Game     O International / CL / EL

O National Team     O Practice Game     O Test-/Pre Season Game

| Items | Me | Coach | | Average |
|---|---|---|---|---|
| Tactical implementation | | | | |
| Selfactivating / Power | | | | |
| Focus / Concentration | | | | |
| Courageous, self-confident action | | | | |
| Fighting Spirit | | | | |
| Competition setting | | | | |
| Action / handling security | | | | |
| Mental stability | | | | |
| Body language | | | | |
| Pause effectiveness | | | | |
| | | | | |
| | | | | |
| | | | | |
| | | | | |
| **Mental Score** / Average | | | | |

**Important comments**

**Goal(s) for the upcoming training week**

**Goal(s) for the upcoming game/competition**

# Game / Competition 13 _____

Date: _____ Play time: _____ H/Min

O League Game   O Cup Game   O International / CL / EL

O National Team   O Practice Game   O Test-/Pre Season Game

| Items | Me | Coach | Average |
|---|---|---|---|
| Tactical implementation | | | |
| Selfactivating / Power | | | |
| Focus / Concentration | | | |
| Courageous, self-confident action | | | |
| Fighting Spirit | | | |
| Competition setting | | | |
| Action / handling security | | | |
| Mental stability | | | |
| Body language | | | |
| Pause effectiveness | | | |
| | | | |
| | | | |
| | | | |
| | | | |
| **Mental Score / Average** | | | |

**Important comments**

**Goal(s) for the upcoming training week**

**Goal(s) for the upcoming game/competition**

# Game / Competition 14 _____

Date: _____        Play time: _____ H/Min

O League Game    O Cup Game    O International / CL / EL

O National Team    O Practice Game    O Test-/Pre Season Game

| Items | Me | Coach | | Average |
|---|---|---|---|---|
| Tactical implementation | | | | |
| Selfactivating / Power | | | | |
| Focus / Concentration | | | | |
| Courageous, self-confident action | | | | |
| Fighting Spirit | | | | |
| Competition setting | | | | |
| Action / handling security | | | | |
| Mental stability | | | | |
| Body language | | | | |
| Pause effectiveness | | | | |
| | | | | |
| | | | | |
| | | | | |
| | | | | |
| **Mental Score / Average** | | | | |

© HeikoHansen.de

**Important comments**

**Goal(s) for the upcoming training week**

**Goal(s) for the upcoming game/competition**

# Game / Competition 15 _____

Date: _____     Play time: _____ H/Min

O League Game    O Cup Game    O International / CL / EL

O National Team    O Practice Game    O Test-/Pre Season Game

| Items | Me | Coach | | Average |
|---|---|---|---|---|
| Tactical implementation | | | | |
| Selfactivating / Power | | | | |
| Focus / Concentration | | | | |
| Courageous, self-confident action | | | | |
| Fighting Spirit | | | | |
| Competition setting | | | | |
| Action / handling security | | | | |
| Mental stability | | | | |
| Body language | | | | |
| Pause effectiveness | | | | |
| | | | | |
| | | | | |
| | | | | |
| | | | | |
| **Mental Score / Average** | | | | |

       © HeikoHansen.de

**Important comments**




**Goal(s) for the upcoming training week**




**Goal(s) for the upcoming game/competition**

# Game / Competition 16 _____

Date: _____    Play time: _____ H/Min

O League Game    O Cup Game    O International / CL / EL

O National Team    O Practice Game    O Test-/Pre Season Game

| Items | Me | Coach | Average |
|---|---|---|---|
| Tactical implementation | | | |
| Selfactivating / Power | | | |
| Focus / Concentration | | | |
| Courageous, self-confident action | | | |
| Fighting Spirit | | | |
| Competition setting | | | |
| Action / handling security | | | |
| Mental stability | | | |
| Body language | | | |
| Pause effectiveness | | | |
| | | | |
| | | | |
| | | | |
| | | | |
| **Mental Score /** Average | | | |

© HeikoHansen.de

**Important comments**

**Goal(s) for the upcoming training week**

**Goal(s) for the upcoming game/competition**

# Game / Competition 17 _____

Date: _____  Play time: _____ H/Min

O League Game   O Cup Game   O International / CL / EL

O National Team   O Practice Game   O Test-/Pre Season Game

| Items | Me | Coach | | Average |
|---|---|---|---|---|
| Tactical implementation | | | | |
| Selfactivating / Power | | | | |
| Focus / Concentration | | | | |
| Courageous, self-confident action | | | | |
| Fighting Spirit | | | | |
| Competition setting | | | | |
| Action / handling security | | | | |
| Mental stability | | | | |
| Body language | | | | |
| Pause effectiveness | | | | |
| | | | | |
| | | | | |
| | | | | |
| | | | | |
| **Mental Score / Average** | | | | |

**Important comments**

**Goal(s) for the upcoming training week**

**Goal(s) for the upcoming game/competition**

# Game / Competition 18 _____

Date: _____       Play time: _____ H/Min

O League Game      O Cup Game      O International / CL / EL

O National Team      O Practice Game      O Test-/Pre Season Game

| Items | Me | Coach | | Average |
|---|---|---|---|---|
| Tactical implementation | | | | |
| Selfactivating / Power | | | | |
| Focus / Concentration | | | | |
| Courageous, self-confident action | | | | |
| Fighting Spirit | | | | |
| Competition setting | | | | |
| Action / handling security | | | | |
| Mental stability | | | | |
| Body language | | | | |
| Pause effectiveness | | | | |
| | | | | |
| | | | | |
| | | | | |
| | | | | |
| **Mental Score / Average** | | | | |

**Important comments**

**Goal(s) for the upcoming training week**

**Goal(s) for the upcoming game/competition**

# Game / Competition 19 _____

Date: _____        Play time: _____ H/Min

O League Game    O Cup Game    O International / CL / EL

O National Team    O Practice Game    O Test-/Pre Season Game

| Items | Me | Coach | | Average |
|---|---|---|---|---|
| Tactical implementation | | | | |
| Selfactivating / Power | | | | |
| Focus / Concentration | | | | |
| Courageous, self-confident action | | | | |
| Fighting Spirit | | | | |
| Competition setting | | | | |
| Action / handling security | | | | |
| Mental stability | | | | |
| Body language | | | | |
| Pause effectiveness | | | | |
| | | | | |
| | | | | |
| | | | | |
| | | | | |
| **Mental Score** / Average | | | | |

## Important comments

## Goal(s) for the upcoming training week

## Goal(s) for the upcoming game/competition

# Game / Competition 20 _____

Date: _____      Play time: _____ H/Min

O League Game     O Cup Game     O International / CL / EL

O National Team     O Practice Game     O Test-/Pre Season Game

| Items | Me | Coach | | Average |
|---|---|---|---|---|
| Tactical implementation | | | | |
| Selfactivating / Power | | | | |
| Focus / Concentration | | | | |
| Courageous, self-confident action | | | | |
| Fighting Spirit | | | | |
| Competition setting | | | | |
| Action / handling security | | | | |
| Mental stability | | | | |
| Body language | | | | |
| Pause effectiveness | | | | |
| | | | | |
| | | | | |
| | | | | |
| | | | | |
| **Mental Score / Average** | | | | |

**Important comments**

**Goal(s) for the upcoming training week**

**Goal(s) for the upcoming game/competition**

# Game / Competition 21 _____

Date: _____     Play time: _____ H/Min

O League Game     O Cup Game     O International / CL / EL

O National Team     O Practice Game     O Test-/Pre Season Game

| Items | Me | Coach | | Average |
|---|---|---|---|---|
| Tactical implementation | | | | |
| Selfactivating / Power | | | | |
| Focus / Concentration | | | | |
| Courageous, self-confident action | | | | |
| Fighting Spirit | | | | |
| Competition setting | | | | |
| Action / handling security | | | | |
| Mental stability | | | | |
| Body language | | | | |
| Pause effectiveness | | | | |
| | | | | |
| | | | | |
| | | | | |
| | | | | |
| **Mental Score / Average** | | | | |

**Important comments**




**Goal(s) for the upcoming training week**




**Goal(s) for the upcoming game/competition**

# Game / Competition 22 _____

Date: _____          Play time: _____ H/Min

O League Game     O Cup Game     O International / CL / EL

O National Team     O Practice Game     O Test-/Pre Season Game

| Items | Me | Coach | | Average |
|---|---|---|---|---|
| Tactical implementation | | | | |
| Selfactivating / Power | | | | |
| Focus / Concentration | | | | |
| Courageous, self-confident action | | | | |
| Fighting Spirit | | | | |
| Competition setting | | | | |
| Action / handling security | | | | |
| Mental stability | | | | |
| Body language | | | | |
| Pause effectiveness | | | | |
| | | | | |
| | | | | |
| | | | | |
| | | | | |
| **Mental Score / Average** | | | | |

**Important comments**

**Goal(s) for the upcoming training week**

**Goal(s) for the upcoming game/competition**

# Game / Competition 23 _____

Date: _____        Play time: _____ H/Min

O League Game    O Cup Game    O International / CL / EL

O National Team    O Practice Game    O Test-/Pre Season Game

| Items | Me | Coach | | Average |
|---|---|---|---|---|
| Tactical implementation | | | | |
| Selfactivating / Power | | | | |
| Focus / Concentration | | | | |
| Courageous, self-confident action | | | | |
| Fighting Spirit | | | | |
| Competition setting | | | | |
| Action / handling security | | | | |
| Mental stability | | | | |
| Body language | | | | |
| Pause effectiveness | | | | |
| | | | | |
| | | | | |
| | | | | |
| | | | | |
| **Mental Score / Average** | | | | |

© HeikoHansen.de

**Important comments**

**Goal(s) for the upcoming training week**

**Goal(s) for the upcoming game/competition**

# Game / Competition 24 _____

Date: _____     Play time: _____ H/Min

O League Game     O Cup Game     O International / CL / EL

O National Team     O Practice Game     O Test-/Pre Season Game

| Items | Me | Coach | | Average |
|---|---|---|---|---|
| Tactical implementation | | | | |
| Selfactivating / Power | | | | |
| Focus / Concentration | | | | |
| Courageous, self-confident action | | | | |
| Fighting Spirit | | | | |
| Competition setting | | | | |
| Action / handling security | | | | |
| Mental stability | | | | |
| Body language | | | | |
| Pause effectiveness | | | | |
| | | | | |
| | | | | |
| | | | | |
| | | | | |
| **Mental Score / Average** | | | | |

**Important comments**

**Goal(s) for the upcoming training week**

**Goal(s) for the upcoming game/competition**

# Game / Competition 25 _____

Date: _____     Play time: _____ H/Min

O League Game     O Cup Game     O International / CL / EL

O National Team     O Practice Game     O Test-/Pre Season Game

| Items | Me | Coach | | Average |
|---|---|---|---|---|
| Tactical implementation | | | | |
| Selfactivating / Power | | | | |
| Focus / Concentration | | | | |
| Courageous, self-confident action | | | | |
| Fighting Spirit | | | | |
| Competition setting | | | | |
| Action / handling security | | | | |
| Mental stability | | | | |
| Body language | | | | |
| Pause effectiveness | | | | |
| | | | | |
| | | | | |
| | | | | |
| | | | | |
| **Mental Score / Average** | | | | |

© HeikoHansen.de

**Important comments**

**Goal(s) for the upcoming training week**

**Goal(s) for the upcoming game/competition**

# Game / Competition 26 _____

Date: _____          Play time: _____ H/Min

O League Game      O Cup Game      O International / CL / EL

O National Team      O Practice Game      O Test-/Pre Season Game

| Items | Me | Coach | | Average |
|---|---|---|---|---|
| Tactical implementation | | | | |
| Selfactivating / Power | | | | |
| Focus / Concentration | | | | |
| Courageous, self-confident action | | | | |
| Fighting Spirit | | | | |
| Competition setting | | | | |
| Action / handling security | | | | |
| Mental stability | | | | |
| Body language | | | | |
| Pause effectiveness | | | | |
| | | | | |
| | | | | |
| | | | | |
| | | | | |
| **Mental Score / Average** | | | | |

**Important comments**

**Goal(s) for the upcoming training week**

**Goal(s) for the upcoming game/competition**

# Game / Competition 27 _____

Date: _____     Play time: _____ H/Min

O League Game     O Cup Game     O International / CL / EL

O National Team     O Practice Game     O Test-/Pre Season Game

| Items | Me | Coach | | Average |
|---|---|---|---|---|
| Tactical implementation | | | | |
| Selfactivating / Power | | | | |
| Focus / Concentration | | | | |
| Courageous, self-confident action | | | | |
| Fighting Spirit | | | | |
| Competition setting | | | | |
| Action / handling security | | | | |
| Mental stability | | | | |
| Body language | | | | |
| Pause effectiveness | | | | |
| | | | | |
| | | | | |
| | | | | |
| | | | | |
| **Mental Score / Average** | | | | |

**Important comments**

**Goal(s) for the upcoming training week**

**Goal(s) for the upcoming game/competition**

# Game / Competition 28 _____

Date: _____  Play time: _____ H/Min

O League Game    O Cup Game    O International / CL / EL

O National Team    O Practice Game    O Test-/Pre Season Game

| Items | Me | Coach | | Average |
|---|---|---|---|---|
| Tactical implementation | | | | |
| Selfactivating / Power | | | | |
| Focus / Concentration | | | | |
| Courageous, self-confident action | | | | |
| Fighting Spirit | | | | |
| Competition setting | | | | |
| Action / handling security | | | | |
| Mental stability | | | | |
| Body language | | | | |
| Pause effectiveness | | | | |
| | | | | |
| | | | | |
| | | | | |
| | | | | |
| **Mental Score / Average** | | | | |

**Important comments**

**Goal(s) for the upcoming training week**

**Goal(s) for the upcoming game/competition**

# Game / Competition 29 _____

Date: _____          Play time: _____ H/Min

○ League Game     ○ Cup Game     ○ International / CL / EL

○ National Team     ○ Practice Game     ○ Test-/Pre Season Game

| Items | Me | Coach | | Average |
|---|---|---|---|---|
| Tactical implementation | | | | |
| Selfactivating / Power | | | | |
| Focus / Concentration | | | | |
| Courageous, self-confident action | | | | |
| Fighting Spirit | | | | |
| Competition setting | | | | |
| Action / handling security | | | | |
| Mental stability | | | | |
| Body language | | | | |
| Pause effectiveness | | | | |
| | | | | |
| | | | | |
| | | | | |
| | | | | |
| **Mental Score / Average** | | | | |

© HeikoHansen.de

**Important comments**




**Goal(s) for the upcoming training week**




**Goal(s) for the upcoming game/competition**

# Game / Competition 30 _____

Date: _____       Play time: _____ H/Min

O League Game     O Cup Game     O International / CL / EL

O National Team     O Practice Game     O Test-/Pre Season Game

| Items | Me | Coach | | Average |
|---|---|---|---|---|
| Tactical implementation | | | | |
| Selfactivating / Power | | | | |
| Focus / Concentration | | | | |
| Courageous, self-confident action | | | | |
| Fighting Spirit | | | | |
| Competition setting | | | | |
| Action / handling security | | | | |
| Mental stability | | | | |
| Body language | | | | |
| Pause effectiveness | | | | |
| | | | | |
| | | | | |
| | | | | |
| | | | | |
| **Mental Score / Average** | | | | |

© HeikoHansen.de

**Important comments**

**Goal(s) for the upcoming training week**

**Goal(s) for the upcoming game/competition**

# Game / Competition 31 _____

Date: _____    Play time: _____ H/Min

O League Game    O Cup Game    O International / CL / EL

O National Team    O Practice Game    O Test-/Pre Season Game

| Items | Me | Coach | | Average |
|---|---|---|---|---|
| Tactical implementation | | | | |
| Selfactivating / Power | | | | |
| Focus / Concentration | | | | |
| Courageous, self-confident action | | | | |
| Fighting Spirit | | | | |
| Competition setting | | | | |
| Action / handling security | | | | |
| Mental stability | | | | |
| Body language | | | | |
| Pause effectiveness | | | | |
| | | | | |
| | | | | |
| | | | | |
| | | | | |
| **Mental Score** / Average | | | | |

**Important comments**

**Goal(s) for the upcoming training week**

**Goal(s) for the upcoming game/competition**

# Game / Competition 32 _____

Date: _____      Play time: _____ H/Min

O League Game     O Cup Game     O International / CL / EL

O National Team     O Practice Game     O Test-/Pre Season Game

| Items | Me | Coach | | Average |
|---|---|---|---|---|
| Tactical implementation | | | | |
| Selfactivating / Power | | | | |
| Focus / Concentration | | | | |
| Courageous, self-confident action | | | | |
| Fighting Spirit | | | | |
| Competition setting | | | | |
| Action / handling security | | | | |
| Mental stability | | | | |
| Body language | | | | |
| Pause effectiveness | | | | |
| | | | | |
| | | | | |
| | | | | |
| | | | | |
| **Mental Score / Average** | | | | |

© HeikoHansen.de

**Important comments**

**Goal(s) for the upcoming training week**

**Goal(s) for the upcoming game/competition**

# Game / Competition 33 _____

Date: _____ Play time: _____ H/Min

O League Game   O Cup Game   O International / CL / EL

O National Team   O Practice Game   O Test-/Pre Season Game

| Items | Me | Coach | | Average |
|---|---|---|---|---|
| Tactical implementation | | | | |
| Selfactivating / Power | | | | |
| Focus / Concentration | | | | |
| Courageous, self-confident action | | | | |
| Fighting Spirit | | | | |
| Competition setting | | | | |
| Action / handling security | | | | |
| Mental stability | | | | |
| Body language | | | | |
| Pause effectiveness | | | | |
| | | | | |
| | | | | |
| | | | | |
| | | | | |
| **Mental Score / Average** | | | | |

**Important comments**

**Goal(s) for the upcoming training week**

**Goal(s) for the upcoming game/competition**

# Game / Competition 34 _____

Date: _____          Play time: _____ H/Min

O League Game     O Cup Game     O International / CL / EL

O National Team     O Practice Game     O Test-/Pre Season Game

| Items | Me | Coach | | Average |
|---|---|---|---|---|
| Tactical implementation | | | | |
| Selfactivating / Power | | | | |
| Focus / Concentration | | | | |
| Courageous, self-confident action | | | | |
| Fighting Spirit | | | | |
| Competition setting | | | | |
| Action / handling security | | | | |
| Mental stability | | | | |
| Body language | | | | |
| Team spirit | | | | |
| | | | | |
| | | | | |
| | | | | |
| | | | | |
| **Mental Score / Average** | | | | |

© HeikoHansen.de

**Important comments**

**Goal(s) for the upcoming training week**

**Goal(s) for the upcoming game/competition**

# Game / Competition 35 _____

Date: _____        Play time: _____ H/Min

○ League Game    ○ Cup Game    ○ International / CL / EL

○ National Team    ○ Practice Game    ○ Test-/Pre Season Game

| Items | Me | Coach | | Average |
|---|---|---|---|---|
| Tactical implementation | | | | |
| Selfactivating / Power | | | | |
| Focus / Concentration | | | | |
| Courageous, self-confident action | | | | |
| Fighting Spirit | | | | |
| Competition setting | | | | |
| Action / handling security | | | | |
| Mental stability | | | | |
| Body language | | | | |
| Pause effectiveness | | | | |
| | | | | |
| | | | | |
| | | | | |
| | | | | |
| **Mental Score / Average** | | | | |

© HeikoHansen.de

**Important comments**

**Goal(s) for the upcoming training week**

**Goal(s) for the upcoming game/competition**

# Game / Competition 36 _____

Date: _____     Play time: _____ H/Min

O League Game     O Cup Game     O International / CL / EL

O National Team     O Practice Game     O Test-/Pre Season Game

| Items | Me | Coach | | Average |
|---|---|---|---|---|
| Tactical implementation | | | | |
| Selfactivating / Power | | | | |
| Focus / Concentration | | | | |
| Courageous, self-confident action | | | | |
| Fighting Spirit | | | | |
| Competition setting | | | | |
| Action / handling security | | | | |
| Mental stability | | | | |
| Body language | | | | |
| Pause effectiveness | | | | |
| | | | | |
| | | | | |
| | | | | |
| | | | | |
| **Mental Score** / Average | | | | |

**Important comments**

**Goal(s) for the upcoming training week**

**Goal(s) for the upcoming game/competition**

# Game / Competition 37 _____

Date: _____ Play time: _____ H/Min

O League Game   O Cup Game   O International / CL / EL

O National Team   O Practice Game   O Test-/Pre Season Game

| Items | Me | Coach | | Average |
|---|---|---|---|---|
| Tactical implementation | | | | |
| Selfactivating / Power | | | | |
| Focus / Concentration | | | | |
| Courageous, self-confident action | | | | |
| Fighting Spirit | | | | |
| Competition setting | | | | |
| Action / handling security | | | | |
| Mental stability | | | | |
| Body language | | | | |
| Pause effectiveness | | | | |
| | | | | |
| | | | | |
| | | | | |
| | | | | |
| **Mental Score / Average** | | | | |

**Important comments**

**Goal(s) for the upcoming training week**

**Goal(s) for the upcoming game/competition**

# Game / Competition 38 _____

Date: _____  Play time: _____ H/Min

O League Game   O Cup Game   O International / CL / EL

O National Team   O Practice Game   O Test-/Pre Season Game

| Items | Me | Coach | | Average |
|---|---|---|---|---|
| Tactical implementation | | | | |
| Selfactivating / Power | | | | |
| Focus / Concentration | | | | |
| Courageous, self-confident action | | | | |
| Fighting Spirit | | | | |
| Competition setting | | | | |
| Action / handling security | | | | |
| Mental stability | | | | |
| Body language | | | | |
| Pause effectiveness | | | | |
| | | | | |
| | | | | |
| | | | | |
| | | | | |
| **Mental Score / Average** | | | | |

© HeikoHansen.de

**Important comments**




**Goal(s) for the upcoming training week**




**Goal(s) for the upcoming game/competition**

# Game / Competition 39 _____

Date: _____ 　　 Play time: _____ H/Min

O League Game 　 O Cup Game 　 O International / CL / EL

O National Team 　 O Practice Game 　 O Test-/Pre Season Game

| Items | Me | Coach | | Average |
|---|---|---|---|---|
| Tactical implementation | | | | |
| Selfactivating / Power | | | | |
| Focus / Concentration | | | | |
| Courageous, self-confident action | | | | |
| Fighting Spirit | | | | |
| Competition setting | | | | |
| Action / handling security | | | | |
| Mental stability | | | | |
| Body language | | | | |
| Pause effectiveness | | | | |
| | | | | |
| | | | | |
| | | | | |
| | | | | |
| **Mental Score / Average** | | | | |

　　　　　　　　　　　　　　© HeikoHansen.de

**Important comments**

**Goal(s) for the upcoming training week**

**Goal(s) for the upcoming game/competition**

# Game / Competition 40 _____

Date: _____ Play time: _____ H/Min

O League Game    O Cup Game    O International / CL / EL

O National Team    O Practice Game    O Test-/Pre Season Game

| Items | Me | Coach | | Average |
|---|---|---|---|---|
| Tactical implementation | | | | |
| Selfactivating / Power | | | | |
| Focus / Concentration | | | | |
| Courageous, self-confident action | | | | |
| Fighting Spirit | | | | |
| Competition setting | | | | |
| Action / handling security | | | | |
| Mental stability | | | | |
| Body language | | | | |
| Pause effectiveness | | | | |
| | | | | |
| | | | | |
| | | | | |
| | | | | |
| **Mental Score / Average** | | | | |

**Important comments**




**Goal(s) for the upcoming training week**




**Goal(s) for the upcoming game/competition**

# Game / Competition 41 _____

Date: _____          Play time: _____ H/Min

O League Game     O Cup Game     O International / CL / EL

O National Team   O Practice Game   O Test-/Pre Season Game

| Items | Me | Coach | | Average |
|---|---|---|---|---|
| Tactical implementation | | | | |
| Selfactivating / Power | | | | |
| Focus / Concentration | | | | |
| Courageous, self-confident action | | | | |
| Fighting Spirit | | | | |
| Competition setting | | | | |
| Action / handling security | | | | |
| Mental stability | | | | |
| Body language | | | | |
| Pause effectiveness | | | | |
| | | | | |
| | | | | |
| | | | | |
| | | | | |
| **Mental Score / Average** | | | | |

**Important comments**

**Goal(s) for the upcoming training week**

**Goal(s) for the upcoming game/competition**

# Game / Competition 42 _____

Date: _____     Play time: _____ H/Min

O League Game    O Cup Game    O International / CL / EL

O National Team    O Practice Game    O Test-/Pre Season Game

| Items | Me | Coach | | Average |
|---|---|---|---|---|
| Tactical implementation | | | | |
| Selfactivating / Power | | | | |
| Focus / Concentration | | | | |
| Courageous, self-confident action | | | | |
| Fighting Spirit | | | | |
| Competition setting | | | | |
| Action / handling security | | | | |
| Mental stability | | | | |
| Body language | | | | |
| Pause effectiveness | | | | |
| | | | | |
| | | | | |
| | | | | |
| | | | | |
| **Mental Score / Average** | | | | |

© HeikoHansen.de

**Important comments**

**Goal(s) for the upcoming training week**

**Goal(s) for the upcoming game/competition**

# Game / Competition 43 _____

Date: _____     Play time: _____ H/Min

○ League Game     ○ Cup Game     ○ International / CL / EL

○ National Team     ○ Practice Game     ○ Test-/Pre Season Game

| Items | Me | Coach | | Average |
|---|---|---|---|---|
| Tactical implementation | | | | |
| Selfactivating / Power | | | | |
| Focus / Concentration | | | | |
| Courageous, self-confident action | | | | |
| Fighting Spirit | | | | |
| Competition setting | | | | |
| Action / handling security | | | | |
| Mental stability | | | | |
| Body language | | | | |
| Pause effectiveness | | | | |
| | | | | |
| | | | | |
| | | | | |
| | | | | |
| **Mental Score / Average** | | | | |

© HeikoHansen.de

**Important comments**

**Goal(s) for the upcoming training week**

**Goal(s) for the upcoming game/competition**

# Game / Competition 44 _____

Date: _____     Play time: _____ H/Min

O League Game     O Cup Game     O International / CL / EL

O National Team     O Practice Game     O Test-/Pre Season Game

| Items | Me | Coach | | Average |
|---|---|---|---|---|
| Tactical implementation | | | | |
| Selfactivating / Power | | | | |
| Focus / Concentration | | | | |
| Courageous, self-confident action | | | | |
| Fighting Spirit | | | | |
| Competition setting | | | | |
| Action / handling security | | | | |
| Mental stability | | | | |
| Body language | | | | |
| Pause effectiveness | | | | |
| | | | | |
| | | | | |
| | | | | |
| | | | | |
| **Mental Score** / Average | | | | |

**Important comments**

**Goal(s) for the upcoming training week**

**Goal(s) for the upcoming game/competition**

# Game / Competition 45 _____

Date: _____     Play time: _____ H/Min

O League Game     O Cup Game     O International / CL / EL

O National Team     O Practice Game     O Test-/Pre Season Game

| Items | Me | Coach | | Average |
|---|---|---|---|---|
| Tactical implementation | | | | |
| Selfactivating / Power | | | | |
| Focus / Concentration | | | | |
| Courageous, self-confident action | | | | |
| Fighting Spirit | | | | |
| Competition setting | | | | |
| Action / handling security | | | | |
| Mental stability | | | | |
| Body language | | | | |
| Pause effectiveness | | | | |
| | | | | |
| | | | | |
| | | | | |
| | | | | |
| **Mental Score / Average** | | | | |

**Important comments**




**Goal(s) for the upcoming training week**




**Goal(s) for the upcoming game/competition**

# Game / Competition 46 _____

Date: _____     Play time: _____ H/Min

O League Game    O Cup Game    O International / CL / EL

O National Team    O Practice Game    O Test-/Pre Season Game

| Items | Me | Coach | | Average |
|---|---|---|---|---|
| Tactical implementation | | | | |
| Selfactivating / Power | | | | |
| Focus / Concentration | | | | |
| Courageous, self-confident action | | | | |
| Fighting Spirit | | | | |
| Competition setting | | | | |
| Action / handling security | | | | |
| Mental stability | | | | |
| Body language | | | | |
| Pause effectiveness | | | | |
| | | | | |
| | | | | |
| | | | | |
| | | | | |
| **Mental Score / Average** | | | | |

© HeikoHansen.de

**Important comments**

**Goal(s) for the upcoming training week**

**Goal(s) for the upcoming game/competition**

# Game / Competition 47 _____

Date: _____          Play time: _____ H/Min

O League Game     O Cup Game     O International / CL / EL

O National Team     O Practice Game     O Test-/Pre Season Game

| Items | Me | Coach | | Average |
|---|---|---|---|---|
| Tactical implementation | | | | |
| Selfactivating / Power | | | | |
| Focus / Concentration | | | | |
| Courageous, self-confident action | | | | |
| Fighting Spirit | | | | |
| Competition setting | | | | |
| Action / handling security | | | | |
| Mental stability | | | | |
| Body language | | | | |
| Pause effectiveness | | | | |
| | | | | |
| | | | | |
| | | | | |
| | | | | |
| **Mental Score / Average** | | | | |

© HeikoHansen.de

**Important comments**


**Goal(s) for the upcoming training week**


**Goal(s) for the upcoming game/competition**

# Game / Competition 48 _____

Date: _____        Play time: _____ H/Min

○ League Game    ○ Cup Game    ○ International / CL / EL

○ National Team    ○ Practice Game    ○ Test-/Pre Season Game

| Items | Me | Coach | Average |
|---|---|---|---|
| Tactical implementation | | | |
| Selfactivating / Power | | | |
| Focus / Concentration | | | |
| Courageous, self-confident action | | | |
| Fighting Spirit | | | |
| Competition setting | | | |
| Action / handling security | | | |
| Mental stability | | | |
| Body language | | | |
| Pause effectiveness | | | |
| | | | |
| | | | |
| | | | |
| | | | |
| **Mental Score / Average** | | | |

© HeikoHansen.de

**Important comments**




**Goal(s) for the upcoming training week**




**Goal(s) for the upcoming game/competition**

# NOTES / MEMO